Grandmother, I Want to Hear Your Story

A Grandmother's Guided Journal To Share Her Life & Her Love

Jeffrey Mason

Hear Your Story

"Everything

I am,

you helped me

to be."

— Author Unknown

THIS BOOK BELONGS TO:

_____

_____

"GRANDMOTHERS AND ROSES ARE MUCH THE SAME. EACH IS GOD'S MASTERPIECE WITH DIFFERENT NAMES."

– AUTHOR UNKNOWN

About This Book

"The thing that interests me most about family history
is the gap between the things we think we know
about our families and the realities." – Jeremy Hardy

Our families are our connections to what came before and what comes after. They show us the magnificence of what can happen when we set aside our own needs, ignore our differences, and allow ourselves to join with others.

Our connections with each other are strengthened when we hear and understand each other's life stories and "Grandmother, I Want to Hear Your Story" provides a place for some of the best storytellers of all to share their lives and their experiences.

Hearing who they are and where they have been allows us to see them in new ways.

We see them as girls growing into young women and as women holding on to some of who they were as little girls. We see their stumbles and their triumphs, and we learn from their challenges and their chosen paths.

We see how alike we are, we better understand and empathize, and we develop new perspectives on our differences, beliefs and judgments.

"Grandmother, I Want to Hear Your Story" is a book dedicated to the timeless and sacred art of passing on, sharing, and learning from the collective stories of our families.

IT'S YOUR BIRTHDAY!
"Life began with waking up and loving my mother's face."
— George Eliot

What is your birthdate?

_____

What was your full name at birth?

_____

Were you named after a relative or someone else of significance?

_____

_____

_____

In what city were you born?

_____

What was your length and weight at birth?

_____

Were you born in a hospital? If not, where?

_____

_____

Was your birth early, on-time, or late?

_____

_____

IT'S YOUR BIRTHDAY!
"Grandmas are moms with lots of frosting."
— Author Unknown

How old were your parents when you were born?

_____

_____

How old were you when you took your first steps?

_____

What were your first words?

_____

_____

How did your parents describe you as a baby?

_____

_____

_____

_____

_____

_____

_____

_____

IT'S YOUR BIRTHDAY!
"The great use of life is to spend it for
something that will outlast it." — William James

What stories have you been told about the day you were
born?

_____

_____

_____

_____

_____

_____

_____

_____

_____

_____

_____

_____

_____

IT'S YOUR BIRTHDAY!

"It's such a grand thing to be a mother of a mother – that's why the world calls her grandmother." — Author Unknown

What is a favorite childhood memory?

_____

_____

_____

_____

_____

_____

_____

_____

_____

_____

_____

_____

_____

WHAT HAPPENED THE YEAR YOU WERE BORN?

"As I learned from growing up, you don't
mess with your grandmother." — Prince William

Google the following for the year you were born:
What are some notable events that occurred?

_____

_____

_____

_____

What movie won the Academy Award for Best Picture?

_____

Who won for Best Actor and Best Actress?

_____

What were a few popular movies that came out that year?

_____

_____

_____

_____

WHAT HAPPENED THE YEAR YOU WERE BORN?

"The most important thing in the
world is family and love." — John Wooden

What song was on the top of the Billboard charts?

_____

Who was the leader of the country (President, Prime
Minister, etc.)?

_____

What were a few popular television shows?

_____

_____

_____

_____

_____

What were the prices for the following items?
- A loaf of bread:
- A gallon of milk:
- A cup of coffee:
- A dozen eggs:
- The average cost of a new home:
- A first-class stamp:
- A new car:
- A gallon of gas:
- A movie ticket:

GROWING UP

"We are born of love; love is our mother."
— Rumi

How would you describe yourself when you were a kid?

_____

_____

_____

_____

Did you have a nickname when you were growing up? If yes, how did you get it?

_____

Who were your best friends in your elementary school days? Are you still in contact with them?

_____

_____

_____

_____

_____

_____

_____

_____

GROWING UP

"Every house needs a grandmother in it."
— Louisa May Alcott

What were your regular chores? Did you get an allowance?
How much was it and what did you spend it on?

_____

_____

_____

_____

_____

What was a typical Saturday like when you were a kid?
What did you spend the day doing?

_____

_____

_____

_____

_____

_____

_____

GROWING UP
"A grandma's heart is a patchwork of love."
— Author Unknown

Describe what your room looked like when you were growing up. Did you share it? Was it messy or clean? Did you have paintings or posters on the walls? What were the main colors?

_____

_____

_____

_____

_____

_____

_____

_____

_____

_____

_____

_____

_____

GROWING UP
"If nothing is going well, call your grandmother."
— Italian Proverb

What is one thing you miss about being a kid?

_____

_____

_____

_____

_____

_____

_____

_____

_____

_____

_____

_____

_____

GRANDMOTHER TRIVIA

"A mind that is stretched by a new experience can never
go back to its old dimensions." — Oliver Wendell Holmes

What is your favorite flavor of ice cream?

_____

How do you like your coffee?

_____

_____

If you could live anywhere in the world for a year with all
expenses paid, where would you choose?

_____

_____

_____

How do you like your eggs cooked?

_____

Preference: cook or clean?

_____

What is your shoe size?

_____

How old were you when you got your first email address?

_____

_____

GRANDMOTHER TRIVIA

"Just about the time a woman thinks her work is done,
she becomes a grandmother." — Edward H. Dreschnack

What is your favorite flower or plant?

_____

_____

What is your biggest fear?

_____

_____

Is there a dish you've perfected over the years and love to cook? (If you wish to share the recipe, there is room in the back of the book to write it down.)

_____

_____

_____

What would you order as your last meal?

_____

_____

_____

_____

_____

_____

THE TEENAGE YEARS

"Families are like branches on a tree. We grow in different directions, yet our roots remain as one." — Author Unknown

How would you describe yourself when you were a teenager?

_____

_____

_____

_____

_____

_____

_____

How did you dress and style your hair during your teens?

_____

_____

_____

_____

_____

_____

_____

THE TEENAGE YEARS

"Teenagehood – that time in life when you show your
individuality by looking like everyone else." — Author Unknown

Did you hang out with a group or just a few close friends?
Are you still close with any of them?

_____

_____

_____

_____

_____

Describe a typical Friday or Saturday night during your
high school years.

_____

_____

_____

_____

_____

_____

_____

THE TEENAGE YEARS
"Little children, headache; big children, heartache."
— Italian Proverb

Did you have a curfew?

_____

_____

Was there a time you got in trouble for getting in past
your curfew? If yes, what were you doing? What was your
punishment?

_____

_____

_____

_____

_____

_____

_____

_____

_____

_____

_____

THE TEENAGE YEARS

"Keep true to the dreams of your youth."
— Friedrich Schiller

Did you date during your high school years?

_____

_____

Did you go to any school dances? What were they like?

_____

_____

_____

_____

Who taught you to drive and in what kind of car?

_____

_____

How old were you when you got your first car? What kind of car was it (year, make, and model)?

_____

_____

What were your grades like?

_____

_____

_____

THE TEENAGE YEARS
"Having a teenager can cause parents to wonder
about each other's heredity." — Author Unknown

Did you have a favorite subject and a least favorite?

_____

_____

_____

What did you like and dislike about high school?

_____

_____

_____

_____

_____

What school activities or sports did you participate in?

_____

_____

_____

_____

_____

THE TEENAGE YEARS

"Life is a winding path through hills and valleys and in
the end, the journey is all that matters." — Author Unknown

What are a few favorite songs from your high school years?

_____

_____

_____

_____

_____

_____

_____

_____

_____

_____

_____

_____

_____

_____

THE TEENAGE YEARS
"Family is the most important thing in the world."
— Diana, Princess of Wales

Knowing all you know now, what advice would you give to your teenage self? What might you have done differently in school if you knew then what you know now?

_____

_____

_____

_____

_____

_____

_____

_____

_____

_____

_____

_____

_____

THE TEENAGE YEARS

"The most important thing in the world is family and love."
— John Wooden

Write about a teacher, coach, or other mentor who had a significant impact on you when you were growing up.

_____

_____

_____

_____

_____

_____

_____

_____

_____

_____

_____

_____

_____

BEGINNINGS

"We don't stop going to school when we graduate."
— Carol Burnett

What did you do after high school? Did you get a job, go to college or a trade school, or become a mother? Something else?

_____

_____

_____

_____

Why did you make this choice?

_____

_____

_____

_____

_____

If you went to college or trade school, what was your major/the focus of your education?

_____

_____

_____

BEGINNINGS
"it takes courage to grow up and become who you really are"
— ee cummings

How did this time period impact who you are today?

_____

_____

_____

_____

_____

If you could go back, what, if anything, would you change about this period of your life? Why?

_____

_____

_____

_____

_____

_____

_____

WORK & CAREER

"Even if you're on the right track, you'll get
run over if you just sit there." — Will Rogers

When you were a kid, what did you want to be when you grew up?

_____

_____

What was your first job? How old were you? How much were you paid?

_____

_____

How many jobs have you had during your lifetime? List a few of your favorites.

_____

_____

_____

_____

_____

What is your least favorite job you have had?

_____

_____

_____

WORK & CAREER

"I'm a great believer in luck, and I find the
harder I work, the more I have of it." — Thomas Jefferson

Is there a job or profession your parents wanted you to
pursue? What was it?

_____

_____

_____

When people ask you what profession you are/were in, your
response is...

_____

_____

_____

How did you get into this career?

_____

_____

_____

_____

_____

_____

WORK & CAREER

"Choose a job you love and you will never
have to work a day in your life." — Confucius

What are/were the best parts of this profession?

_____

_____

_____

_____

_____

_____

_____

What aspects did you or do you dislike about it?

_____

_____

_____

_____

_____

WORK & CAREER

"If people knew how hard I worked to get my mastery,
it wouldn't seem so wonderful after all." — Michelangelo

Who was the best boss you ever had? Why were they such
a good manager?

_____

_____

_____

_____

_____

What are some of your work and career-related
achievements that you are proudest of?

_____

_____

_____

_____

_____

_____

_____

GRANDMOTHER TRIVIA

"Even though you're growing up, you
should never stop having fun." — Nina Dobrev

What name would you choose if you had to change your
first name?

_____

What is a memory of a time when you got in trouble when
you were young? What happened? What was your
punishment?

_____

_____

_____

_____

_____

_____

_____

_____

_____

_____

_____

_____

GRANDMOTHER TRIVIA

"Grandparents, like heroes, are as necessary
to a child's growth as vitamins." — Joyce Allston

How old were you when your family got their first
television?

_____

What is your favorite way to relax?

_____

_____

_____

Have you ever been told that you look like someone famous?
If yes, who?

_____

Did you ever skip school? If yes, did you get away with it
and what did you do during the time you should have been
in class?

_____

_____

_____

_____

_____

_____

FAMILY TREE
"Each of us is tomorrow's ancestors."
— Author Unknown

My Great-Grandmother
(My Grandmother's Mom)

My Great-Grandmother
(My Grandfather's Mom)

My Great-Grandfather
(My Grandmother's Dad)

My Great-Grandfather
(My Grandfather's Dad)

My Grandmother
(My Mom's Mom)

My Grandfather
(My Mom's Dad)

My Mother

FAMILY TREE

"As you do for your ancestors, your children will do for you."
— African Proverb

_____
My Great-Grandmother
(My Grandmother's Mom)

_____
My Great-Grandmother
(My Grandfather's Mom)

_____
My Great-Grandfather
(My Grandmother's Dad)

_____
My Great-Grandfather
(My Grandfather's Dad)

_____
My Grandmother
(My Dad's Mom)

_____
My Grandfather
(My Dad's Dad)

_____
My Father

PARENTS & GRANDPARENTS

"When all the dust is settled and all the crowds are gone, the
things that matter are faith, family, and friends." — Barbara Bush

Where was your mother born and where did she grow up?

_____

_____

_____

How would you describe her?

_____

_____

_____

In what ways are you most like your mother?

_____

_____

_____

_____

_____

_____

_____

_____

PARENTS & GRANDPARENTS

"Education is what remains after one has forgotten
what one has learned in school." — Albert Einstein

Where was your father born and where did he grow up?

_____

_____

_____

How would you describe him?

_____

_____

_____

In what ways are you most like your father?

_____

_____

_____

_____

_____

_____

_____

_____

PARENTS & GRANDPARENTS
"A moment lasts for seconds but the memory of it lasts forever."
— Author Unknown

What is a favorite memory of your mother?

_____

_____

_____

_____

_____

_____

_____

_____

_____

_____

_____

_____

_____

_____

PARENTS & GRANDPARENTS
"We don't remember days, we remember moments."
— Author Unknown

What is a favorite memory of your father?

_____

_____

_____

_____

_____

_____

_____

_____

_____

_____

_____

_____

_____

_____

PARENTS & GRANDPARENTS

"To forget one's ancestors is to be a brook without
a source, a tree without a root." — Chinese Proverb

What was your mother's maiden name?

_____

Do you know from what part(s) of the world your
mother's family originates?

_____

_____

_____

Do you know your father's mother's maiden name?

_____

_____

Do you know from what part(s) of the world your father's
family originates?

_____

_____

_____

How did your parents meet?

_____

_____

_____

PARENTS & GRANDPARENTS
"Grandmas hold our tiny hands for just a little while...
but our hearts forever." — Author Unknown

How would you describe their relationship?

_____

_____

_____

_____

_____

What were your parents' occupations?

_____

_____

_____

_____

Did either of them have any unique talents or skills?

_____

_____

_____

_____

Did either of them serve in the military?

_____

PARENTS & GRANDPARENTS

"Love is the chain whereby to bind a child to its parents."
— Abraham Lincoln

What is a favorite family tradition that was passed down from your parents or grandparents?

_____

_____

_____

What are a few of your favorite things that your mother or father would cook for the family?

_____

_____

_____

_____

What were your grandparents like on your mother's side?

_____

_____

_____

_____

_____

_____

PARENTS & GRANDPARENTS

"Next to God, thy parents."
— William Penn

Do you know where your mother's parents were born and grew up?

_____

_____

_____

_____

What were your grandparents like on your father's side?

_____

_____

_____

_____

_____

Do you know where your father's parents were born and grew up?

_____

_____

_____

PARENTS & GRANDPARENTS
"Grandparents make the world...a little softer,
a little kinder, a little warmer." — Author Unknown

What is some of the best advice your mother gave you?

_____

_____

_____

_____

_____

_____

_____

_____

_____

_____

_____

_____

_____

_____

PARENTS & GRANDPARENTS

"A father's goodness is higher than the mountain,
a mother's goodness deeper than the sea." — Japanese Proverb

What is some of the best advice your father gave you?

_____

_____

_____

_____

_____

_____

_____

_____

_____

_____

_____

_____

_____

_____

_____

PARENTS & GRANDPARENTS
"My fathers planted for me, and I planted for my children."
— Hebrew Saying

Did you ever meet your great-grandparents on either side
of your family? If yes, what were they like?

_____

_____

_____

_____

_____

_____

_____

_____

_____

_____

_____

_____

_____

PARENTS & GRANDPARENTS
"The longest road out is the shortest road home."
— Irish Proverb

What other individuals had a major role in helping you
grow up?

_____

_____

_____

_____

_____

_____

_____

_____

_____

_____

_____

_____

YOUR SIBLINGS
"Brothers and sisters are as close as hands and feet."
— Vietnamese Saying

Are you an only child, or do you have siblings?

_____

Are you the oldest, middle, or youngest?

_____

List your siblings' names in order of their ages. Make sure to include yourself.

_____

_____

_____

_____

_____

Growing up, which of your siblings were you the closest with?

_____

_____

Which of your siblings are you the closest with in your adult years?

_____

_____

YOUR SIBLINGS

"The greatest gift our parents ever gave us was each other."
— Author Unknown

How would you describe each of your siblings when they were kids?

_____

_____

_____

_____

_____

How would you describe each of your siblings as adults?

_____

_____

_____

_____

_____

_____

YOUR SIBLINGS

"First a brother, then a bother, now a friend."
— Author Unknown

In the following pages, share some favorite memories of each of your siblings. If you're an only child, feel free to share memories of close friends or cousins.

_____

_____

_____

_____

_____

_____

_____

_____

_____

_____

_____

_____

YOUR SIBLINGS

"What causes sibling rivalry? Having more than one kid."
— Tim Allen

Memories...

_____

_____

_____

_____

_____

_____

_____

_____

_____

_____

_____

_____

YOUR SIBLINGS

"Siblings know how to push each other's buttons, but they also
know how to mend things faster than anyone." — Unknown

Memories...

_____

_____

_____

_____

_____

_____

_____

_____

_____

_____

_____

_____

YOUR SIBLINGS

"The advantage of growing up with siblings is that
you become very good at fractions." — Author Unknown

Memories...

_____

_____

_____

_____

_____

_____

_____

_____

_____

_____

_____

_____

_____

BECOMING & BEING A MOM

"Having somewhere to go is home. Having someone to
love is family. Having both is a blessing." — Author Unknown

How old were you when you first became a mother?

_____

What was your favorite part about being pregnant?

_____

_____

_____

_____

_____

What difficulties did you have with your pregnancies, if any?

_____

_____

_____

_____

_____

_____

BECOMING & BEING A MOM

"Being a mom is the answer to every question. She is
our why, who, what and when." — Author Unknown

Were your deliveries early, late, or on-time?

_____

_____

_____

_____

Did you have any food cravings? If yes, what were they?

_____

_____

_____

_____

_____

What were your children's lengths and weights at birth?

_____

_____

_____

_____

BECOMING & BEING A MOM

"The only rock I know that stays steady, the only
institution I know that works, is the family." — Lee Iacocca

Is there a special song you would sing or play to your
children when they were little?

_____

_____

How did having children impact your professional life?

_____

_____

_____

_____

What are the biggest differences in how kids are raised
today and when you were young?

_____

_____

_____

_____

_____

_____

_____

BECOMING & BEING A MOM

"A man's work is from sun to sun, but
a mother's work is never done." — Author Unknown

Looking back, what would you change about how your kids were brought up, if anything?

_____

_____

_____

_____

_____

_____

_____

_____

_____

_____

_____

_____

_____

_____

BECOMING & BEING A MOM

"When I was a boy, I thought my grandmother lived in the kitchen.
The stove was her kingdom, her church, and her medicine cabinet."
— Author Unknown

What are the best and hardest parts of being a mother?

_____

_____

_____

_____

_____

_____

_____

_____

_____

_____

_____

_____

_____

BECOMING & BEING A MOM

"The mother is the one supreme asset of national life; she is more important by far than the successful statesman, or businessman, or artist, or scientist." — Theodore Roosevelt

Write about a favorite memory of being a mother.

_____

_____

_____

_____

_____

_____

_____

_____

_____

_____

_____

_____

_____

BECOMING & BEING A MOM

"Pretty much all the honest truth telling there is in
the world is done by children." — Oliver Wendell Holmes

Knowing what you know now, what advice would you give
yourself as a new mom?

_____

_____

_____

_____

_____

_____

_____

_____

_____

_____

_____

_____

_____

_____

BECOMING & BEING A MOM

"Becoming a mother makes you realize you
can do almost anything one-handed." — Author Unknown

Based upon all you have learned and experienced, what
advice would you give your children?

_____

_____

_____

_____

_____

_____

_____

_____

_____

_____

_____

_____

_____

LET'S TALK ABOUT YOUR KIDS

"Children have one kind of silliness, as you know,
and grown-ups have another kind." — C.S. Lewis

What would your kids have been named if they were born the opposite gender?

_____

_____

_____

_____

Who did they most look like when they were babies?

_____

_____

_____

_____

What were their first words?

_____

_____

_____

_____

_____

LET'S TALK ABOUT YOUR KIDS

"Just when you think you know love, something little comes along and reminds you just how big it is." — Author Unknown

How old were they when they took their first steps?

_____

_____

_____

Were any of your children "surprises?"

_____

_____

_____

Are there any specific books you remember reading to your kids?

_____

_____

_____

_____

When your kids were little, what trick did you use to calm them when they were upset?

_____

_____

_____

LET'S TALK ABOUT YOUR KIDS

"Adults are just outdated children."
— Dr. Seuss

In what ways are your kids like you?

_____

_____

_____

_____

_____

_____

_____

_____

_____

_____

_____

_____

_____

LET'S TALK ABOUT YOUR KIDS

"Study the past, if you would divine the future."
— Confucius

How are they different?

_____

_____

_____

_____

_____

_____

_____

_____

_____

_____

_____

_____

_____

_____

_____

LET'S TALK
ABOUT YOUR GRANDKIDS

"Grandparents are a delightful blend of laughter, caring deeds, wonderful stories, and love." — Author Unknown

How old were you when you became a grandmother?

_____

How many grandkids do you have?

_____

What are your grandkids' names and ages?

_____

_____

_____

_____

_____

_____

_____

_____

_____

LET'S TALK
ABOUT YOUR GRANDKIDS

"Unconditional positive regard is rarely given
by anyone except a grandparent." — Author Unknown

How were you told the first time you would be a
grandmother? What was your reaction?

_____

_____

_____

_____

_____

_____

What do you remember about the first time you held your
first grandchild?

_____

_____

_____

_____

_____

_____

LET'S TALK
ABOUT YOUR GRANDKIDS
"The soul is healed by being with children."
— Fyodor Dostoevsky

What is the most surprising thing about being a grandmother?

_____

_____

_____

_____

_____

_____

_____

_____

_____

_____

_____

_____

LET'S TALK
ABOUT YOUR GRANDKIDS

"Grandmother – a wonderful mother with lots of practice."
— Author Unknown

How is being a grandmother different than being a mother?

_____

_____

_____

_____

_____

_____

_____

_____

_____

_____

_____

_____

_____

_____

GRANDMOTHER TRIVIA

"The greatest gifts you can give your children are the roots of
responsibility and the wings of independence." — Denis Waitley

If you could do any one thing for a day, what would it be?

_____

_____

_____

What is your favorite season? What are some things you
love about that time of the year?

_____

_____

_____

What is a smell that reminds you of your childhood? Why?

_____

_____

What do you do better than anyone else in the family?

_____

_____

_____

GRANDMOTHER TRIVIA

"A child cannot have too many people who love
them and want to help them succeed." — Donna Kaylor

What is your favorite dessert?

_____

What is a favorite memory from the last twelve months?

_____

_____

_____

_____

_____

_____

_____

What is your definition of success?

_____

_____

_____

_____

_____

SPIRITUALITY & RELIGION

"We are not human beings having a spiritual experience;
we are spiritual beings having a human experience."
— Pierre Teilhard de Chardin

What do you believe is the purpose of life?

_____

_____

_____

_____

_____

_____

_____

_____

Which has the most impact on our lives: fate or free will?

_____

_____

_____

_____

_____

_____

SPIRITUALITY & RELIGION

"We are not going in circles; we are going upwards.
The path is a spiral; we have already climbed many steps."
— Hermann Hesse, *Siddhartha*

Were your parents religious when you were growing up? If yes, how did they express their spiritual beliefs?

_____

_____

_____

_____

_____

_____

_____

_____

_____

_____

_____

_____

_____

SPIRITUALITY & RELIGION

"Within you there is a stillness and a sanctuary to which you can retreat at any time and be yourself." — Hermann Hesse

If you are religious or spiritual, how have your beliefs and practices changed over the course of your life?

_____

_____

_____

_____

_____

_____

_____

_____

_____

_____

_____

_____

_____

_____

SPIRITUALITY & RELIGION

"What you are is God's gift to you, what you become
is your gift to God." — Hans Urs von Balthasar, *Prayer*

What religious or spiritual practices do you incorporate
into your daily life today, if any?

_____

_____

_____

_____

_____

_____

_____

Do you believe in miracles? Have you experienced one?

_____

_____

_____

_____

_____

_____

SPIRITUALITY & RELIGION

"When you arise in the morning think of what a privilege it
is to be alive, to think, to enjoy, to love." — Marcus Aurelius

What do you do when times are challenging, and you need
to find additional inner strength?

_____

_____

_____

_____

_____

_____

_____

_____

_____

_____

_____

_____

_____

SPIRITUALITY & RELIGION

"Grandma always made you feel she had been waiting to see just you all day and now the day was complete." — Marcy DeMaree

Write about a time you found relief by forgiving someone.

_____

_____

_____

_____

_____

_____

_____

_____

_____

_____

_____

_____

_____

_____

LOVE & ROMANCE
"We are asleep until we fall in love!"
— Leo Tolstoy, *War and Peace*

Do you believe in love at first sight?

_____

_____

_____

Do you believe in soulmates?

_____

_____

_____

How old were you when you had your first kiss?

_____

What age were you when you went on your first date?

_____

Can you remember who it was with and what you did?

_____

_____

_____

_____

_____

LOVE & ROMANCE
"Whatever our souls are made of, his and mine are the same."
— Emily Brontë, *Wuthering Heights*

How old were you when you had your first steady relationship? Who was it with?

_____

How many times in your life have you been in love?

_____

_____

What are some of the most important qualities of a successful relationship?

_____

_____

_____

_____

_____

_____

_____

_____

LOVE & ROMANCE
"We loved with a love that was more than love."
— Edgar Allan Poe, *Annabel Lee*

Did you have any celebrity crushes when you were young?

_____

_____

_____

_____

Were you ever in a relationship with someone your parents
did not approve of?

_____

_____

_____

Have you ever written someone or had someone write you
a love poem or song?

_____

If yes, write a few lines that you may remember.

_____

_____

_____

_____

_____

LOVE & ROMANCE
"Love is a great beautifier."
— Louisa May Alcott, *Little Women*

In what ways do you feel your parents' relationship influenced how you have approached love and marriage?

_____

_____

_____

_____

_____

Write about a favorite romantic moment.

_____

_____

_____

_____

_____

_____

_____

_____

LOVE & ROMANCE

"We don't remember days, we remember moments."
— Author Unknown

How did you meet our Grandfather?

_____

_____

_____

_____

What was your first impression of him?

_____

_____

_____

_____

What is your proposal story?

_____

_____

_____

_____

LOVE & ROMANCE

"Children are the hands by which we take hold of heaven."
— Henry Ward Beecher

What was your wedding like? Where was it held and who was there? Any good wedding day stories?

_____

_____

_____

_____

_____

_____

_____

_____

_____

_____

_____

_____

_____

_____

TRAVEL
"Once a year, go someplace you've never been before."
— Dali Lama

Do you have a valid passport?

_____

How do you feel about cruises?

_____

_____

How do you feel about flying?

_____

What are a few of your favorite places that you've traveled to?

_____

_____

_____

_____

_____

_____

_____

_____

TRAVEL

"Life is short, and the world is wide."
— Author Unknown

What is a favorite travel memory?

_____

_____

_____

_____

_____

_____

_____

_____

_____

_____

_____

_____

_____

_____

_____

TRAVEL BUCKET LIST

"Man cannot discover new oceans unless he has
the courage to lose sight of the shore." — André Gide

List the top 10 places you would visit if money and time
were no concern.

1. _____

_____

2. _____

_____

3. _____

_____

4. _____

_____

5. _____

_____

TRAVEL BUCKET LIST

"The world is a book, and those who do not
travel read only one page." — Saint Augustine

6. _____

_____

7. _____

_____

8. _____

_____

9. _____

_____

10. _____

_____

GRANDMOTHER TRIVIA
"Grandmothers sprinkle stardust over children's lives."
— Author Unknown

What would you title your autobiography?

_____

_____

_____

Do you think you could still pass the written portion of
the driver's test without studying?

_____

What is your favorite color?

_____

What is your favorite quote?

_____

_____

_____

If you could travel through time and had to choose, who
would you meet: your ancestors or your descendants? Why?

_____

_____

_____

_____

GRANDMOTHER TRIVIA
"Gratitude is the sign of noble souls."
— Aesop

What personal or professional accomplishments are you most proud of?

_____

_____

_____

_____

_____

What are five things you are grateful for?

_____

_____

_____

_____

If you were forced to sing karaoke, what song would you perform?

_____

_____

_____

POLITICAL STUFF
"What you teach your children, you also teach their children."
— Author Unknown

Which best describes how you feel about having political discussions:

☐ I would rather not.
☐ I prefer to have them with people whose views match mine.
☐ I love a good debate.

How old were you the first time you voted?

_____

What are the biggest differences in your political views today and when you were in your early twenties?

_____

_____

_____

_____

Have you ever taken part in a march or boycott? What issues, if any, could motivate you to join one?

_____

_____

_____

_____

POLITICAL STUFF
"In politics stupidity is not a handicap."
— Napoleon Bonaparte

When was the last time you voted?

_____

In what ways do you agree and disagree with the political choices of your children's and grandchildren's generations?

_____

_____

_____

_____

_____

_____

If you woke up to find yourself in charge of the country, what are the first three things you would enact or change?

One: _____

_____

Two: _____

_____

Three: _____

_____

MOVIES, MUSIC, TELEVISION, & BOOKS

"If you want a happy ending, that depends, of course, on where you stop your story." — Orson Welles

What movie have you watched the greatest number of times?

_____

_____

What movie or television show can you remember loving when you were a kid?

_____

_____

Who would you cast to play yourself in the movie of your life? How about for the rest of your family?

_____

_____

_____

_____

_____

_____

_____

MOVIES, MUSIC, TELEVISION, & BOOKS

"If at first you don't succeed, try doing it the way
mom told you to in the beginning." — Author Unknown

What are your favorite genres of music?

_____

_____

_____

_____

Which decades had the best music?

_____

_____

_____

_____

What is the first record (or cassette, cd, etc.) you can
remember buying or being given as a gift?

_____

_____

What song do you like today that would make your younger
self cringe?

_____

_____

MOVIES, MUSIC, TELEVISION, & BOOKS

"Grandmothers are just antique little girls."
— Author Unknown

What is a song from your teens that reminds you of a special event or moment?

_____

_____

_____

What song would you pick as the theme song of your life?

_____

_____

_____

What was the first concert you attended? Where was it held and when?

_____

_____

How has your taste in music changed over the years?

_____

_____

_____

_____

MOVIES, MUSIC, TELEVISION, & BOOKS

"Being a mother means that your heart is no longer yours; it wanders wherever your children do." — George Bernard Shaw

What television show from the past do you wish was still on the air?

_____

If you could be cast in any television show or movie, past or present, which one would you choose?

_____

What are some favorite books from your childhood and/or teenage years?

_____

_____

_____

What book or books have majorly impacted the way you think, work, or live your life?

_____

_____

_____

_____

_____

_____

TOP TEN MOVIES
"Grandmas never run out of hugs or cookies."
— Author Unknown

List up to ten of your most favorite movies:

1. _____

2. _____

3. _____

4. _____

5. _____

6. _____

7. _____

8. _____

9. _____

10. _____

TOP TEN SONGS

"The music is not in the notes, but in the silence in between."
— Wolfgang Amadeus Mozart

List up to ten of your most favorite songs:

1. _____

2. _____

3. _____

4. _____

5. _____

6. _____

7. _____

8. _____

9. _____

10. _____

GRANDMOTHER TRIVIA

"Something magical happens when parents turn into grandparents."
— Author Unknown

What is your favorite holiday and why?

_____

_____

_____

_____

_____

Which ten-year period of your life has been your favorite so far and why?

_____

_____

_____

_____

_____

_____

_____

_____

GRANDMOTHER TRIVIA

"Let me love you a little more before you're not little anymore."
— Author Unknown

Who would you invite if you could have dinner with any five people who have ever lived?

_____

_____

_____

_____

_____

What are some of your most favorite books?

_____

_____

_____

_____

_____

_____

_____

_____

ROOM FOR MORE

"The way I see it, if you want the rainbow, you
gotta put up with the rain." — Dolly Parton

The following pages are for you to expand on some of
your answers, to share more memories, write down a few
favorite family recipes, or to write notes to your loved
ones:

_____

_____

_____

_____

_____

_____

_____

_____

_____

_____

_____

_____

_____

ROOM FOR MORE
"When it seems the world can't understand, your
grandmother's there to hold your hand." — Joyce Logan

_____

_____

_____

_____

_____

_____

_____

_____

_____

_____

_____

_____

_____

_____

ROOM FOR MORE
"Life is a flower of which love is the honey."
— Victor Hugo

_____

_____

_____

_____

_____

_____

_____

_____

_____

_____

_____

_____

_____

ROOM FOR MORE
"Life is short, and it is here to be lived."
— Kate Winslet

_____

_____

_____

_____

_____

_____

_____

_____

_____

_____

_____

_____

_____

_____

ROOM FOR MORE

"Life is really simple, but we insist on making it complicated."
— Confucius

_____

_____

_____

_____

_____

_____

_____

_____

_____

_____

_____

_____

_____

ROOM FOR MORE

"A garden of love grows in a grandmother's heart."
— Author Unknown

_____

_____

_____

_____

_____

_____

_____

_____

_____

_____

_____

_____

HEAR YOUR STORY BOOKS

At **Hear Your Story**, we have created a line of books focused on giving each of us a place to tell the unique story of who we are, where we have been, and where we are going.

Sharing and hearing the stories of the people in our lives creates a closeness and understanding, ultimately strengthening our bonds.

Available at Amazon, all bookstores, and HearYourStoryBooks.com

- Mom, I Want to Hear Your Story: A Mother's Guided Journal to Share Her Life & Her Love

- Dad, I Want to Hear Your Story: A Father's Guided Journal to Share His Life & His Love

- Grandfather, I Want to Hear Your Story: A Grandfather's Guided Journal to Share His Life and His Love

- Tell Your Life Story: The Write Your Own Autobiography Guided Journal

- Life Gave Me You; I Want to Hear Your Story: A Guided Journal for Stepmothers to Share Their Life Story

- You Choose to Be My Dad; I Want to Hear Your Story: A Guided Journal for Stepdads to Share Their Life Story

HEAR YOUR STORY BOOKS

- To My Wonderful Aunt, I Want to Hear Your Story: A Guided Journal to Share Her Life and Her Love

- To My Uncle, I Want to Hear Your Story: A Guided Journal to Share His Life and His Love

- Mom, I Want to Learn Your Recipes: A Keepsake Memory Book to Gather and Preserve Your Favorite Family Recipes

- Dad, I Want to Learn Your Recipes: A Keepsake Memory Book to Gather and Preserve Your Favorite Family Recipes

- Grandmother, I Want to Learn Your Recipes: A Keepsake Memory Book to Gather and Preserve Your Favorite Family Recipes

- Grandfather, I Want to Learn Your Recipes: A Keepsake Memory Book to Gather and Preserve Your Favorite Family Recipes

- Aunt, I Want to Learn Your Recipes: A Keepsake Memory Book to Gather and Preserve Your Favorite Family Recipes

- Uncle, I Want to Learn Your Recipes: A Keepsake Memory Book to Gather and Preserve Your Favorite Family Recipes

- To My Girlfriend, I Want to Hear Your Story

- To My Boyfriend, I Want to Hear Your Story

- Mom & Me: Let's Learn Together Journal for Kids

DEDICATION
To My Grandmothers

To Eula Story Mason: to be your grandchild was to be royalty! Each time I smell Juicy Fruit Gum, drink sweet tea, or cook fried chicken, you are there with me. I think of your smile, your delicate laugh, and your irresistible modesty.

You are always perfectly put together...not a hair out of place, a crisp, ironed blouse and matching pastel pants. Never a negative word and always an unwavering love of God.

What is missed at first glance is your quiet strength. You know endurance, you know what matters. You keep moving forward and always make things work.

To Vivian Hensley Niles: as a young boy I knew you as my Granny, not realizing that you were the forerunner of today's modern woman.

You worked and you were an artist in the kitchen. You paid the bills, and you took care of your family. You had a million opinions and you shared them all, fearlessly. You were proudly you.

I am grateful for your example of *work hard but have fun*, and I aspire to match your boldness and your never-stop-stamina. Every pancake I flip, when I work in the garden, and when I listen to Texas Swing, you're there beside me, coffee cup close at hand.

Granny Mason and Granny Niles, I Love You.

ABOUT THE AUTHOR

Jeffrey Mason is the creator and author of the best-selling **Hear Your Story®** line of books and is the founder of the company **Hear Your Story®**.

In response to his own father's fight with Alzheimer's, Jeffrey wrote his first two books, **Mom, I Want to Hear Your Story** and **Dad, I Want to Hear Your Story** in 2019. Since then, he has written and designed over 30 books, been published in four languages, and sold over 300,000 copies worldwide.

Jeffrey is dedicated to spreading the mission that the little things are the big things and that each of us has an incredible life story that needs to be shared and celebrated. He continues to create books that he hopes will guide people to reflect on and share their full life experience, while creating opportunities for talking, listening, learning, and understanding.

Hear Your Story® can be visited at <u>hearyourstorybooks.com</u> and Jeffrey can be contacted for questions, comments, podcasting, speaking engagements, or just a hello at <u>jeffrey.mason@hearyourstory.com</u>.

He would be grateful if you would help people find his books by leaving a review on Amazon. Your feedback helps him get better at this thing he loves.

VIEW THIS BOOK
ON YOUR COMPUTER

We invite you to also check out Hearyourstory.com, where you can answer the questions in this book using your smart phone, tablet, or computer.

Answering the questions online at Hearyourstory.com allows you to write as much as you want, to save your responses and revisit and revise them whenever you wish, and to print as many copies as you need for you and your whole family.

Please note there is a small one-time charge to cover the cost of maintaining the site.

Copyright © 2023 EYP Publishing, LLC, Hear Your Story Books, & Jeffrey Mason

ISBN: 9781085819015